It's Because They Were Black

100 Years of Fraud and Forgery

By
Syl Johnson

Strategic Book Publishing and Rights Co.

Strategic Book Publishing and Rights Co., LLC
USA | Singapore
www.sbpra.net

For information about special discounts for bulk purchases, please contact Strategic Book Publishing and Rights Co., LLC. Special Sales, at bookorder@sbpra.net.

ISBN: 978-1-68235-535-0

Benediction

There was a man named Wallace Thompson. After the Emancipation Proclamation, he and a few slaves were freed and given money to do as they pleased. Wallace was fourteen or fifteen years old at the time. Their previous owner gave them ten dollars apiece. About two and a half miles away from the plantation, they went into a town called Hollis Springs, Mississippi. They didn't know what to do with that ten dollars at their age, so they went back to the plantation and explained to their master that they didn't know what to do and had come back in hopes they would get some guidance.

He told them, "Well, you can stay here, but you gotta go to work, and I'll pay you half of what you make." They were in disbelief, knowing that he meant business. He was a man of his word. There was no fraud or crime to be found from him.

Wallace took the money to his great-grandmother, grandmother, and Henry, his brother. Great-grandmother and Henry took a mattress, unstitched it, and put the money inside before stitching it back up like nothing was amiss.

In the 1920s, everyone was having a good time. White people were spending their money and became broke, but the black people did not, and many of the white folks were affected by the Great Depression.

By this time, my grandpa, Owen, and his three brothers— Joe, Dan, Will—were great workers. They all worked for a man by the name of John Hudson. He had three plantations and was very wealthy. He also had a son, Lynn Hudson. Lynn was in Chicago in the early 1910s, and he ended up finding himself a wife named Annie. They say she was a beautiful woman. They met at a hotel that she was staying at. He was captured by her beauty, but she was no good. Some say she might have had some black in her genes.

John would go on to tell his son to sell part of his land to the Thompson boys. "They are good boys. Go on and sell some of that land to them."

Lynn agreed, and he ended up selling section 24, township 2, range 2 in Marshall County, Mississippi. It was 642 acres of land, but two of those acres were for the cemetery—one acre for the colored and one acre for the white people. He sold it to them in 1916 for $12,800 and gave them six years to pay.

Even though Lynn was a few years older than my grandfather and his brothers, they were like friends. They worked on the plantation together and knew each other well.

The last payment was due in 1922. It was for $3,082.03. As they were good and noble men, my grandfather and his brothers went to the Federal Land

Bank of New Orleans in October of 1921 and took out a $4,000 loan. Now, their payments would be $285 per year. The loan said that they had to make the last payment of the $3,082.03 to get that loan or they wouldn't be able to get a mortgage from the bank for the next thirty-four years. They don't send out second mortgages now, and they didn't do it back then.

Lynn Hudson passed away on January 31, 1922. He had been secretly saying to my granddad before his death, "Sell it back to me, won't you?" He was talking about the land. Lynn told him that he wasn't sure he could have the land after he passed. Owen told him honestly that he wanted that land for his grandchildren.

After Lynn passed away, Annie was still around. She was a beautiful woman, but she couldn't be trusted. She had ways like a no-good white man.

In 1924, Annie told several lies. She took that land. She took my grandfather's land with lies and fraud. The spirit of God is giving me the chance to reveal her lies. She made four notes in the deed. They didn't owe any of the $3,082.03 that they had to pay off, but she wrote down those lies. Otherwise, they wouldn't have been able to obtain that first mortgage from the Federal Land Bank of New Orleans. She kept putting funny things into the deed, falsifying documents, and when she did that, the recorder of the deed added whatever she told them. What that recorder of deeds did was a greedy, sinful, and outright criminal conspiracy. She said that the brothers were in default of the borrowed money and got the deed in place of foreclosure. She was a fraud.

The brothers had no idea about any of the dirty moves she made. She had the deed put into her name and started borrowing a lot of money from Oxford Bank. What the bank officers did in making those crooked loans was unacceptable. Their greed and crimes are unforgivable, and they did it for a few years. The bank should have done a title search. Instead, they went along with her crimes and sinful ways.

Annie skipped town with the money once Oxford Bank caught wind of what she was doing. In my opinion, the president of the bank should have put out a warrant for the arrest of Annie and the recorder of deeds for forgery, fraud, and civil rights violations. Her leaving made Oxford Bank follow through in filing for foreclosure. The judge committed a crime in accepting the foreclosure. Another crime and sin. The government loan was proof, and the judge had seen it, but he still went through with the foreclosure. The county, the state, and Annie Hudson were the reason for the foreclosure. It may have been racketeering. It may have been illegal.

The judge had a receiver for the foreclosure and made them pay rent on their land. They noted that they could have gotten thirty-five more bales of cotton if they had planted earlier in the year. Cotton was selling for $220 per bale on average, but because of Annie, they didn't believe my grandfather and his brothers could pay their rent.

They made my grandfather and his brothers get off the land in 1932. They came with shotguns and the sheriff. They gave them two weeks, and when that day came, they told them they had twelve hours to leave. They were blindsided by the foreclosure. The authorities took their livestock, farming equipment, food, and keys. They had nothing but the clothes on their backs, and by that time, two new families had started working the land.

My grandfather had my father, and he built a home for my siblings, Annie Mae and James Thompson. All they could do was cry. They knew nothing about the recorder of deeds. All they knew was that they were being told to leave. They knew nothing about the greed, fraud, sin, and crimes that were being used against them.

What they also didn't know was that John made sure that his will stated that when one of his daughters turned seventeen and got married, she'd be the owner of the deed and guardian of the trust. He had three daughters, Virginia, Annie, and Sylvia. Virginia got married at seventeen and became the guardian of the estate. In 1934, Virginia sued the bank and Annie, believing that she deserved the land. She knew that what they were doing was crooked, that the judge was crooked, and that committing crimes against the family that had built up the land was wrong.

By now, most of the Thompsons were in Chicago, but some of them were dead. My grandfather died a few months after this. In 1937, Jay Cooper Hurdle, president of the First State Bank, went down to Oxford Bank in Mississippi with $2,500 cash and bought the land. Jay's daughters did what they could to get in touch with Joe in Chicago. The First State Bank tried to meet with Joe, but he wouldn't agree to it. Jay wanted no part in the decision after clearing material and minerals from the land; he wanted to clear up the deed information. His daughter Janice went on to sell the land to the Matthews in Memphis, Tennessee. All Jay did was take the minerals from the land.

She got a loan from Oxford Bank. It was a crooked bank. The bank, the state, and the county are guilty of sin, crime, and conspiracy. They were all in on destroying a black family. They took care of the white folk but didn't want to support the black men who had helped the white men for the previous four hundred years. They didn't care that their crimes, sin, fraud, and greed were hurting black families.

To rectify these issues with me and my family, I just want forty acres. The cemetery can stay. I want a John Deere tractor with all the tools on it. I want a school so that I can teach kids of all races to grow vegetables. I know how, and I want to pass down this knowledge to them. I will be inviting family members who might need space, about sixty-six of them, for the rest of the six hundred acres. And I would want to have rappers (I believe I can get Jay-Z, Kanye West, Snoop, Wu-Tang, and others to come for free, and I will pay the band) and entertainers come out and perform a free show every year on my forty acres. This is a sign that I will give back. A house and a monument will be built of me on the land. After that, we will build a foundation for other people who have had their family's land stolen so that they can reclaim what is rightfully theirs.

I won't bother them anymore once I've received the money for my land from the state and the county. Oxford Bank, First State Bank, the State of Mississippi, and Marshall County need to give me the land and resources that I am owed—the land that my family was owed.

With all of the social injustice we see today surrounding George Floyd and others, it is time to reclaim what is owed to us. My grandfather, his brothers, and my family are the George Floyds of the past. I want the reader to think about this.

Table of Contents

Is It Because I'm Black

by Syl Johnson (1970)

The dark brown shades of my skin only add color to my tears.

That splash against my hollow bones, that rocks my soul.

Looking back over my false dreams that I once knew.

Wondering why my dreams never came true.

Is it because I'm black?

Somebody tell me, what can I do.

Something is holding me back, is it because I'm black?

(repeat)

In this world of no pity I was raised in the ghetto of the city

Momma she worked so hard to earn every penny.

Oh lord

Something is holding me back

Cause. Is it because I'm black

(repeat)

2nd verse:

Like a child stealing his first piece of candy.

That cost. Even in my corner somewhere I got lost

Something is holding me back. I wonder. Is it because I'm black?

Somebody tell me what I can do.

Will I survive or will I die.

Keep on holding me back

Keep on holding on

Keep on picking on me

Keep on holding me back

Keep on holding on, keep on holding me back

Keep on holding be back, I wonder why you do me like that

But you keep on putting your foot on me

But I've got a break away, somehow, some day,

Cause I wanna be somebody so bad, So bad, I wanna be somebody.

I wanna be somebody so bad. But something is holding me back Is it because I'm black?

Is because I'm black... is because I'm black

Something is holding me back,

I want diamond rings and things

Foreword

Growing up as a young girl, despite the many titles he has held, the main thing I've known my dad as is a fighter. He always fights for his life and his art. He fights for those he cares for and for what is right. He's always instilled that fight in me, my sisters, and brother. He became more than just a father in my eyes, in some of my fondest memories of him. As I would sneak down to our basement, I would witness him creating and recording music. In these small moments, I would get exposure to all of his talents and passions when it came to making music. It was always like being in his world and experiencing something that made him happy. Even as I got older, I remembered him making kids go find music that sampled his songs in record stores; his drive was still under him. Seeing him passionate about his artistry shifted my views of him from just my father, to also being a musician and true artist.

He has always shown resilience, strength, and dedication throughout all of his hardships. As a man who was self-taught, it's inspired all of us in our family to be passionate about never being afraid to reach our goals and doing the impossible. Watching him as I grew up, I was reminded that being treated with respect and receiving the credit you deserve isn't always easy but giving up should never be an option. I believe that once he found out that his label didn't know other artists were sampling from him without permission or credit, he believed his best course of action was to do it himself. I think that realization hit my dad that he could be paid for these samples and given the credit he deserved after his first check came from the artist Boss. It started a fire in him to get what he rightfully deserved and worked for. My dad's fight for his music and all the hard work he has put in throughout the decades he has been in the music industry was the driving force for this book.

In researching his roots, he opened all our eyes to just how influential our family line has been. In the past fifteen years, one of the many things my dad ingrained in us is how important it is for him to leave a legacy. The drive in my dad to leave behind a lasting legacy, wealth, and history for his children, grandchildren, and great-grandchildren is seen through the story of his great-grandfather, Wallace, and grandfather, Owen Thompson.

The story of his great-grandfather is unique to our family, but a story that is similar to many of the slaves and ancestors all African Americans have come from. Hearing this story about my ancestors and family has allowed me to be more connected to my roots and more appreciative of the man my father is, his influence on me, my, sisters and brother, and the hard work of those who came before me that have paved the way.

This story is about the fight for reparations our ancestors fought for and we are still fighting for today—a fight that many black people should be fighting for as well. Of all the lessons I've learned from my dad, it is that fighting for what is right is what's important. Learning where you come from and how your ancestors fought for you to be here is why this book and foundation are important to our lives as black people. Black people leaving behind a rich legacy for future black people to experience and cherish is exactly what my dad and the Reclaim Foundation are setting out to do today.

Dr. Syleecia Thompson

Preface

Throughout life we face many battles. Some challenge our morals and others challenge our mentality. The journey my family took started with honest, hard work and ended in tragedy. My family was tricked out of their land by a dishonest woman named Annie; she can only be described as low-down. However, Annie could not pull her schemes off on her own. This book will highlight how the Jim Crow South rallied behind wrongdoing, especially when a beautiful white woman led the request. We all know the story of Emmett Till, winking at a white woman and being beaten and then hanged by a gang of white men later the same day. White women used their innocence to garner reactions out of white men, whether wrong or right. Rarely were they questioned about their truths or intentions, and it is unfortunate my family was a victim of this behavior. Annie spewed her lies to the chancellor of deeds, bankers, town patrons, and others. Her deceit knew no bounds and led to four brothers losing a little over six hundred acres of highly valuable land. According to the documentation, the brothers owned enough to start their own township. They not only lost the land, but the chance for generational wealth was snatched from them. That is a much larger crime to consider when you look back at the history of blacks within this country.

I write this for the purpose of telling their truth and highlighting the impacts of racism to family generations. The same impacts are seen in more subtle ways today, including my own story of stolen music, a story that I will reference within this book for readers to compare the treatment of blacks today versus the time of my ancestors. Those with a conscience will work to correct wrongdoing in any situation, but not all people are prepared or willing to acknowledge any wrongdoing on their end. What is not known to the public sometimes relieves the conscience of the perpetrator. It also allows for lessons to go unlearned because they have not been talked about or exposed to others. This leaves a vicious cycle of mistreatment of an underserved community. This cycle is one I want to break for myself and my family. Sharing my past and present makes me the teacher and allows the opportunity for new, unknown perspectives to come to light through text.

I believe the black family has been displaced from their home, broken apart by slavery, and suppressed from societal growth by discrimination and racism. This same old cycle continues in new ways. Instead of working fields of cotton, black men are locked behind bars like wild beasts. While a black woman may lead a family, she is not a breadwinner equivalent to her white counterparts. The scales remain tipped, and the evidence of how we crept here lies in the historical treatment of black families.

As you read this, I want you to think about how an entire nation can go about righting many wrongs, especially those that come with substantiated evidence. If I can undoubtedly prove that land was stolen and has not been legally transferred to current owners, as an ancestor of that land, am I not owed a patch of it? What is fair if stealing goes uncorrected and discrimination goes unaddressed? In the same way, what is owed to one family may mean taking from another. Society often views rights from the perspective of the innocent, dismissing the original crime. Consequently, I can determine what is right, but the court should also set legal precedent for the sake of all families who were victims of stolen land or any other aggrievance for which proof exists of their rights.

Chapter 1

A Mother's Love

This story begins with a tale from my mother, a tale that turned out to be the true story of my ancestors. The land they were slaves of, worked to buy, and eventually owned was in the end stolen. It is a tale of how one spiteful, racist woman changed a family's destiny forever. My mother's name was Verlie; she was the oldest of three children. I can still remember sitting by her bedside and hearing her say to me to "keep at it, boy." Our time spent by the bedside was always special to me because I heard many stories about my family. Each time I learned something different and felt more connected to my history. My mother had ten kids in her lifetime. When I would hear many of the stories, she'd often refer to the two eldest children, Annie Mae and James, because they were the only children that experienced living on the family land. My father, Sam, built a family house on the property that my mother referred to as "the most beautiful house" in all her stories. My mother would remind me of the grievances committed against our family and encourage me to fight for what is right. She would tell me I was the one who would bring this story to everyone's attention and reclaim what is ours. As any child would, I promised I would do my part to reclaim what was ours. At the time, I was not completely sure how I would do that, but I knew it was a part of my responsibility and my story to tell in the future. In many ways, she passed the torch to me, and now I sit here with my story to tell. My mother said when she first saw me, she knew I was a baby, but I looked like a businessman. Her intuition told her I would bring attention to our stolen land. It wasn't until I really understood the loss my mother experienced because of the family losing their property that I could pick up this torch for her. Back then, birth control didn't exist, so women often bore children even when circumstances were not ideal for a child. My mother and the rest of the family moved back into her parent's house where my mother's two younger brothers, William and Vernon, were still living. Since my mother was the oldest and coming back home, she had to make her space on the floor of the home. During the time of this transition back home, my mother bore two more children, and both died of pneumonia. Howard, who was one year old when he passed on, and Dub made it to about six months. The conditions of the home didn't support a mother with young children sleeping on the floor, but my mother had no choice. In my opinion, all the judges, lawyers, and officers of the court who allowed the family to be removed from their land participated in the murder of the children who couldn't survive the living conditions they were put in.

First, we are not the only family with this story. There are plenty of black families whose lands were stolen from underneath them. Blacks did not have the advantage of reading and writing and knowing the ins and outs of land deeds. However, my family was educated and well known in the community. Annie Mae was a college professor before she died of kidney disease, and James is a famous Blues singer that goes by the name Jimmy Johnson. Although our family could read and write, our knowledge didn't save us from the evil actions of the city officials. There was a reliance on the system treating individuals who bought land fairly. In Holly Springs, Mississippi, fairness was not a part of the law—particularly in Marshall County, where corrupt a government was headquartered and where our land was as well, which brings the second important point. Marshall County had a history of being corrupt. There were chop shops, stolen land, murders, and other mysterious, controversial, blatant illegal dealings within the county. Business dealings in the county often went unquestioned and unchallenged because the government and all of the employees were corrupt. It was better to keep your mouth shut than to risk being a victim of Marshall County law.

As an entertainer, I've evolved with the times, but I am one of the few left that traveled and performed in this business when racism was still blatant. I lived through the changes of the industry and became successful, despite how it is engineered for the artist to fail. My mother looked to me as someone who could get things done. She would say, "Go back to Mississippi and get Grandfather's land back from those crooked white folks that took it." Where I can actually get on my own is left to be seen, but I know that this story and many others must be told. There is land—there is plenty of it—and some may belong to your family.

My Great-Grandfather

"My great-grandfather, Slave Wallace."

Slave Wallace was the father of the Thompson men, four gentlemen you will learn more about in the coming chapters. Wallace was born and raised in Mississippi, and he was a well-known slave on his plantation. The Hudsons were the first known family that owned the land, this may be because of their engagement with the slaves on the land allowed for them to build relationships that initiated the first memories of ownership. Land in Mississippi changed hands often, and all assets go with it. Negros were an asset like cattle; they stayed with the property and the plantation when sold. Wallace was about fourteen years old when he was freed by the Emancipation Proclamation. At that time, he was given ten dollars to go and make a life for himself. Like many other slaves, he had nowhere to go, nowhere to sleep, and no other family to rely on. So, Wallace went back to the plantation to continue to work with the family he had already known and built a relationship with. Wallace had four sons and continued to work on the plantation as a free man for the remainder of his life. These sons would benefit from the work their father put in by becoming owners. Their ownership changed their wealth for generations to come.

The boys were talented beyond measure, often playing a variety of instruments. They would perform at local fish fries and collect a good amount of money from their entertainment gigs. Their talent and ability to entertain was widely known within their small town. This talent was passed down from generation to generation. I am Owen's grandson, Syl Johnson, and I am one of the many in this family that received the music gene. My career has led to world fame as a singer, songwriter, and producer. Carrying on the legacy of the Thompson family and bringing attention to racism through my music has been exciting and, more importantly, gratifying. Learning of the family's deep-rooted history with stolen land, I found similarities in my life that reflected my grandfather's past.

As an up and coming musician, I suffered many grievances at the hands of record labels and industry executives, often finding myself fighting for my music and my rights to acknowledgement and payment. I found solace in being acknowledged by the various music artists who leveraged my work in the past. Some artists established personal relationships, while others continued to honor me with payments and awards. I found my family's history aligned with my personal experience with musical artists today. This made me step up to take a look at my past and attempt to resolve some wrongdoings done to my grandfather and his brothers. Much like my music career, the items stolen leave a trail of evidence, a real-life story of fraud, colluding, lies, and deceit that can only be told best by following the timeline of the past.

"My mother's mother."

Neither side of my family is a stranger to slavery. It is well known that slaves were given land and that most, if not all, had their land taken away after the Emancipation Proclamation because the new leadership in America did not deem them worthy. The promise of wealth or the ability to farm was snatched from many families who would have been successful, given their background of tending to other's lands for decades. My family is one of the few that bought land outright, but despite owing money, having a lien, and banks being involved, they too were not deemed worthy but underhanded by those who should have taken more interest in ensuring laws were not broken. It begs the question, what is fair? If reparations are not accepted and land will not be handed out, then how is it fair to also take land that is bought? Where are the lines drawn for blatant and subtle racism and discrimination?

Many young people of color today do not realize their lack of wealth and ownership is because it was stolen from their ancestors. Most have just chosen to accept that they are of a lower class or participate in this great nation at a different socioeconomic level. The truth is that what we do not know and fail to learn keeps us in this cycle of lacking. If a moment is taken to understand family history and how ancestors were treated, generations can begin to demand justice and change the paradigm of ongoing racism and discrimination.

Chapter 2

Mississippi: The Headquarters of Slavery

There once was a woman named Annie Hudson. She was a beautiful woman, with ways like a no-goodass white man. Annie couldn't be trusted. She devised a super plan to help herself and Jim Crow by taking one black family's land. Her plan worked, as it did for many whites who stole land from blacks. This story, however, is unique, because a paper trail was left behind that can be followed in detail. The land was muscled away from three black brothers who worked hard to obtain it and even harder to maintain it.

The story goes that the four brothers, named Joe, Dan, Will, and Owen Thompson, worked on a plantation for the Hudson family for many years. The men picked cotton for the family and were some of the best slaves the family had known. All three were tall, strong, and quite engaged with the family, which led to a longstanding relationship between the Hudsons and Thompsons.

John Hudson was the owner of the land the men worked on, which was located in Holly Springs,

Mississippi, and had three sections to it. The land owned by Hudson was massive in size, and the sections produced crops, making the Hudson family pretty wealthy and well known in the area. John Hudson had a son named Lynn. He and his father both appeared to be decent and thoughtful overall. Lynn grew close to the brothers, building his own relationship with each of them. Some would say it seemed Lynn had two sides or two spirits. One spirit was towards blacks and Hispanics that showed no judgement. He treated colored people with respect and decency, but his other spirit was jealous and looked down upon them. The side Lynn showed the Thompson brothers was mostly positive. He even taught Owen how to read and write. Owen shared his learning with his younger brother, Joe. Lynn treated Owen like a friend. Owen was the eldest of the brothers and naturally became like a leader to them and the other workers on the Hudson property.

John Hudson witnessed the relationship between Lynn and the brothers. He too saw the Thompsons as special to his family. John instructed his son Lynn to sell the Thompson brothers a section of the land to have for their own. Lynn promised his father he would sell a section of the property. Around 1910, John Hudson passed away and Lynn became the owner of the property. Lynn kept his word to his father, and in 1916, sold the brothers section 24, township 2, range 2 in Marshall County, MS. The land was 642 acres, with two acres dedicated to a cemetery, one acre for colored, and one for whites. The land was large enough to start its own township by county standards. Lynn sold the land to the brothers on contract for $12,800. Per the agreement, the brothers had six years to pay for the land. Payments were $3,000 a year, and the last payment of $3,016.98 was due in 1922. Owen often spoke on behalf of the brothers and took the lead on the transfer of the land from the Hudson's.

After the sale of land, the brothers began to bring in their own income from the cotton on their property. It didn't take long before the brothers were considered wealthy in the neighborhood. Lynn came back to the brothers' time and time again, requesting they sell the land back. At one point, Lynn increased the amount to buy it back to over double what he had sold it for initially. It appeared that Lynn may have known something about the land, which led to him wanting to get it back desperately. When asked, Lynn gave a variety of reasons why he wanted the land back. He often stated he was afraid the men wouldn't be able to keep up with the cost after he was gone. If Lynn died, he wanted to make sure the land was safe and given to his grandson. Lynn's concerns for the brother's ability to pay didn't make much sense, because the brothers were paying as agreed and the years were flying by. Moreover, the land was full of cotton, more than enough to pay for the brother's cost and leave room for a little extra. The year 1922 rolled around quickly.

That was the year the land was to be paid off by the brothers, and so it was. Prior to the new year, Owen went to the Federal Bank of New Orleans and got a loan against the land for $4,000. This money paid off the outstanding loan to the Hudson family and took first lien position. The difference in funds was given to the brothers in October of 1921. The federal loan deed stated there couldn't be any liens or any incumbent upon the land during the thirty years of repayment. The repayment amount was around $285 a year, which was a very small payment in comparison to the $2,500 a year the brothers had maintained previously. The brothers were pretty much in the clear and owned their land outright, with just one lien to the Federal Bank of New Orleans outstanding.

On January 31, 1922, Lynn passed away. He was thirty years older than Annie Hudson, his wife. They had three daughters together, Virginia, Sylvia, and Annie. In his will, the two sections of land his family still owned were split between his daughters, and some went to his son from a previous relationship. The eldest daughter, Virginia, was expected to become the executor of the estate when she turned seventeen and got married. Her guardianship would override her mother, Annie, who was the temporary guardian of the estate until the time came. Annie took full advantage of her guardianship of the land Lynn left behind. She also took it upon herself to get back the sold portions. The scheme Annie put together includes accusations, lies,

laws of ownership. The land was slid from under them, and they were too naive and uneducated to fight for their rights. The brothers took this as a loss, and the entire family retreated to other states with other family. Life went on, but as times changed, it became more and more apparent that there was fraud, dishonesty, and a corrupt government involved. To make matters worse, the foreclosure was not the end of the story.

While all the families were displaced from their land, Virginia was approaching age of guardianship in 1934. She was living with Annie in Chicago at Al Capone's hotel, the Sutherland Hotel. This hotel was well known for the riffraff that came through it. You could find bank robbers, pickpockets, and others who were not abiding by the law in this hotel. One would assume Annie's scheme to acquire previously sold land through the means that she used may have been perpetuated by the criminals she was surrounded by during her stay in Chicago. Her daughter Virginia took issue with her about the land and her business decisions as guardian. In 1934, Virginia and her husband sued Oxford Bank, and Annie, for the land to be returned. Annie had previously sold everything on the land and received loans on the land as the guardian, making a mess of the financials. Virginia argued that she was the rightful guardian, and the loans and sale of property should have never taken place until she came of age.

The state and the county agreed with Virginia's argument and reversed the deeds back to the original owner, Lynn, who, according to his will, appointed Virginia as owner. All land was reversed, except the Thompson land. This was likely because the original owner was not Lynn, as the land had been sold prior to his death. Consequently, Virginia was granted two sections of the land back, while the Thompson brothers received nothing in the ruling. It was clear Annie had no authority to take loans out on the Thompson land or foreclose on them because it was not owned by the Hudson's, but the land still was not included in the reversal decision by the court. The court didn't acknowledge the section owned by the Thompsons and didn't return it to Virginia as part of the reversal. Annie, who had recorded multiple documents against the Thompson land while working with her buddies in the recorder's office, had seemingly succeeded in tricking everyone involved in her scheme. Trick is a kind word, considering no one that assisted her questioned the validity of her claims or contacted the brothers to verify information.

Virginia was made whole in her transaction, receiving everything her father had left her and beginning her life again. The Thompson land at this point had a very complicated chain of title that was illegally broken.

Chapter 4

A Sample of the Past

I am a multi-talented genius. My story goes back to a time when racism and discrimination were still played out on the public stage of life. Although it is not entirely eradicated, it is not as overt today as it was during the highs of my career. I found solace in traveling abroad. I toured Russia and found the people to be wonderful to me despite my skin color. One night, myself and the band were playing. We headed up to the stadium and found our entry to be especially difficult. As a musical artist, the last thing you think about is getting into your venue to play for the thousands waiting on you. We learned Putin had decided to come to the show, and the additional security was for his protection. After waiting for a little over an hour to get in and get setup, we hit the stage to perform for a little over eight thousand that night. The audience was aware of Putin's presence, and they were in rare form that night. It was arguably one of the best performance nights I have ever had in my career.

This led to wanting to produce my album *Live in Russia*, which is in the works now. Russia will always hold a special place for me because of the unique and high-energy experience I had there. Not long after leaving Russia, I performed at Moscow Forum for thirty days and the year prior toured most of Turkey. There were many seven- and eight-year-old abandoned children throughout Turkey. These visuals put things into perspective for me. I was there for over forty days and can vividly remember the homeless children I encountered.

My career is a myriad of these experiences lumped into one memory of existence. I still sing the tunes that depict the heartaches and souls of not only the country I live in but of those I visited. My soul music became a broader depiction of the highs and lows we all feel throughout our journeys. I used this sound and separated myself as a musician in America on the Chitlin' Circuit.

The Chitlin' Circuit was below the Mason-Dixon line—Mississippi, Alabama, Tennessee, Arkansas, Florida, Louisiana, Texas, and the Carolinas. This is where I, Syl Johnson, was a household name. I traveled the circuit and knew the cost. There were hotels I could not stay in, so I slept in shacks and rooms offered by friends and fans on the tour path. There were restaurants that I could not eat at because I was black. This is where the concept of chicken shacks came from, because the same homes that offered their beds would sell chicken to travelers. I wasn't alone in this circuit. Many famous artists went through it, like the Supremes, the Temptations, and Gladys Knight. We all had our time of sleeping on the bus and eating at a shack. I became well known on the circuit and soon built a routine that carried me and my band through the Deep South.

A few years later, the circuit started to die out as disco became the main attraction. This was also the time DJs were being pushed out of radio stations. Radio wanted less chatter and more clatter. The race to be the best radio station meant playing the latest and biggest hits the most. As DJs were pushed out, blues, R&B, soul and funk music were lost in the shuffle. Music started to focus in on dance moves. Shake your tail feather, the twist, kill that roach, monkey time, and funky Broadway became popular dances. The era of music and dance was upon us, and it was fun for all the artists involved, but it didn't change that we still had no rights and could not eat at the same places most of our fans enjoyed.

I didn't mind not eating in places we were not wanted, because it was well known that servers or cooks would spit in black's food. So, it was much easier to make the choice to have soul food from a trusted friend or someone who looked like me. During this time, the travel started to slow down as a result of the music fading away. The economy was experiencing a gas crisis, and disc jockeys were leaving radio. I began to settle into a calmer life, but it didn't stay that way for long.

My personal story of stolen music mirrors that of my family's stolen land, but like Virginia, I have been made whole by many of the artists who have sampled my music. Sampling music is one way newer artists are able to use well-known or popular melodies. My music has been sampled over 350 times across more than six genres of music. From hip-hop to rock, pop, blues, soul, and country, melodies I created have been ingrained in some of your favorite songs. This has taken my career to new levels, because work previously established continues to be relevant and generate income for me and my family. However, the outcome I am experiencing now did not come easy.

I fought for my music. Record labels attempted to steal my masters, while some artists used melodies and never reached out for permission or payment to me. Most people negotiated once approached by my legal team, but a few ended up in court, with ongoing cases today. No one, including myself, wants to be tied up in court for years when one payment can rectify the situation. With all that said, for me it was never about the money. I get the most pleasure from the accolades and acknowledgement. Sharing in the success of a song and receiving a plaque for my contributions is meaningful to me. Just as acknowledgement of wrongdoing by Annie Hudson and many of the county workers, along with a piece of the original land, would have been meaningful to Owen and his brothers.

"Syl Johnson press clipping for Japan."

Chapter 5

Syleena Johnson

My daughter, Syleena, wanted to sing. I was completely against it for her, because I knew the lifestyle of singers. I have seen it all during my own career, so I was cautious for my child. Despite my caution, she was adamant about singing and went forward with getting her own band put together.

I entertained her impromptu performance by making an appearance at one of their practice sessions. I said to Syleena, "SING! Let me hear you!"

Syleena belted out "My Funny Valentine" with ease, so I challenged her to sing something harder, with higher notes. "Do a Whitney Houston song."

Syleena started singing "Saving All my Love for You." I was stunned, but now I wanted to understand her range. I told her to "sing Anita Baker." Syleena belted out "Caught Up in the Rapture," and she killed it. I was sold on helping her, but right away I learned the doors that I had access to worked a little different for women.

Syleena had to always go through a doorman, A&R and a few others, before even getting her voice heard. During this time, a guy from Mississippi stepped in to help out with her career. Syleena was given a beat by the gentleman, and within minutes, while the music was still playing, Syleena wrote "So Confused." I knew then she was brilliant. She could sing and write her own music.

I took her to Joy Art Studios. Syleena sang in the lounge at the studio, which overlooked a glassed-off area where patrons could sit and listen to singers as they record and practice. When Syleena was finished, the people in the lounge gave her a standing ovation. Her light was brighter than even I could expect.

Charles Everett was a good friend of mine, and he owned a club along with a hundred-thousand-watt radio station, WMPR. I had played in his club and was a well-known artist on his radio station. I considered him a friend and knew his family history, as he did mine. Charles's brother, Medgar Evers, was an NAACP leader and one of the first blacks to integrate a Mississippi college. His efforts to stop the Jim Crow South led to him being shot in his driveway. He is one of many stories that reminds us of how harsh the times were then to have an opinion or be a smart black man making strides. Charles was similar to his brother, but his popularity was in a different circuit, maybe one not so threatening to the segregated South. I knew if I could get him to play Syleena's song in the club and on the station, word would spread about her like wildfire. So, I engaged him and introduced Syleena to him.

Charles sent us through his Uncle Bobo, who liked Syleena and wanted to help. This is where promo man Senator Jones came into the picture. Senator was a nighttime DJ who was known for playing soul and blues music. Senator took a chance on Syleena and played one of her songs on the radio, but he didn't get much of a reaction from his audience, as he expected. Syleena during this time had an EP with a few songs on it, but her clear hit was "So Confused." Senator's wife convinced him to play Syleena one more time and this time play "So Confused." Senator played it, and the boards of the station lit up with requests to play more. People were looking to buy the record right away. Senator called me about two weeks later and told me this was the best record he had played in maybe ten years. He needed copies to sell.

During that time, I had about ten thousand copies of Syleena's EP in my car. My car had so many records that there was only space for one person to ride, and that was my driver's seat. I had just given up on the records and even attempted to throw them away a week prior. I had taken a few boxes to the garbage, and the garbage man asked me if he could have one. I said sure, and his buddy comes from around the truck and asked for one too. They began talking about how pretty Syleena was and how she looked like she could sing. We had a good laugh about it, then the driver of the garbage truck yelled out the window that he wanted one. I took that as a sign it wasn't time to throw them away, and it's a good thing I didn't. Senator asked for all the copies I had and paid me before every shipment. I sent them all to the station in Mississippi.

After about three weeks, the records were all gone, and I couldn't print or sell anymore because Syleena had a record deal. Syleena's record company was not moving on releasing any music from her, but her popularity on the southern stations and growing fan base forced them to take her off the shelf.

Today, Syleena stills sings and is an international star, as am I. I believe I am more well known in other countries outside of the US, but Syleena seems to have a large US base. Her music career took a slightly different journey than my own, but she too values and understands why we must fight to keep the things our ancestors worked hard to get. Syleena went to school to study nutrition and has built her own company, teaching and sharing information on how to live a better life with food. How wonderful would it be for her to have land to grow fruits and vegetables as our ancestors once did, and as I once did?

Sometimes I wonder, what if the stockholders of Oxford Bank read this book and were enlightened to the thievery that took place? Would they attempt to make it right? Calling out wrongdoing is within our right to do, but how do we make it right for the person, family or history that has been wronged? I believe it is through acknowledgement and the attempt to restore what was lost that things can be corrected. By using our voices, we can continue to push this conversation of righting the wrongs bestowed upon our ancestors and us today. My family is not the only family who has had land stolen. In the South, the practice of taking land from black owners was as common as the practice of taking music from artists is today.

What people may not know is that any melody created by an artist first becomes their personal property. Leveraging that melody, even in an altered state, requires permission of the owner. My music set the tone to many rap albums, and well-known artists have continued to utilize some of the original music I created today, but not all artists are created equal. What should appear easy and clear cut has been an ongoing struggle. I choose to fight for what belongs to me. However, many artists are not as willing to do the same. The cost to fight too many cases sometimes feels like it is not worth it. However, not fighting is an injustice to all artists who create beautiful music, in the same way not fighting for my grandfather's land would be amiss to all families who have had land outright stolen from them.

The evidence for my music and for the land is in writing and can be followed by anyone that chooses to take a look at the documentation. In the same way, forty acres seems like a fair gesture at a minimum to recoup what was taken, a place to build a monument to the brothers who had their land stolen from them, an attempt to acknowledge blacks as owners and builders of the modern world we live in today. It is the lack of rectification and retribution that has left many black families poor. At what point will something be paid by the perpetrators who broke laws to keep blacks out of ownership?

Chapter 6
Copyrights

The copyright laws do not allow an artist to re-loop a song and call it their own. Many young artists don't know this truth, and it has taken multiple court cases and some general understanding of artistry to protect my work. Time and time again, many other artists have had to protect theirs as well. Today, I own all the rights to my music, and there is no record label that is able to distribute my music without my knowledge. This was the case with Jefferson Airplane, a group that moved forward with their song "You Wear Your Dresses Too Short," which was a rendition of my song "Dresses Too Short." The group thought that since the words were not exact, the song was not considered under copyright laws. However, altering copyrights to make a new version of the same song is still covered under copyright law. We went to court over the issue and I won.

I have learned that the modernization of music technology has made it much easier to reuse and repeat previous work. Technology today can loop four beats into a thousand beats for a new melody. Biz Markie re-looped two or three of my beats, altering the original copyright, which again opened the door for me to challenge ownership. Even an altered beat is still stolen, and the government will recognize that without issue. I would think the same would go for someone that has altered a deed. If it was music, the owner who did the altering is subject to criminal prosecution, or they can settle out of court and pay the cost to use the original beat. As an artist who has over three hundred samples, you can start to paint a picture of how many times this has been done to me—some in good conscious and others that resulted in legal battles have occurred for me. Most settled out of court, but the concept of fighting for property is not new to me. I have worked with some of the biggest artist of our time, and many have sampled my music on their own. Some of my work includes:

Michael Jackson – "Blood on the Dance Floor"

NWA – "Fight the Power"

WuTang Clan – "Shame on a N*****"

Big Daddy Kane – "Dancing with the Devil"

Ghetto Boys – "Homie Don't Play That"

Kwame – "Only You"

Snoop Dogg – "Because I'm Black"

Kid Rock – "Cowboy"

Speaking of Kid Rock, he is an example of an artist that made a wrong right. Not only did Kid Rock acknowledge the use of the beat, he also stepped forward to ensure I received the proper accolades for my contribution to the record.

"Syl's gold record with Ghostface Killah"

"Syl's collection of gold records with various artist"

"Syl is writer/producer 11 times platinum with Kid Rock"

"Syl is acknowledged by Wutang for his involvement in the album"

"Syl receives acknowledgement from Wutang and Erik and Rakim for his work on the album"

"Syl surrounded by accolades"

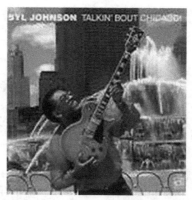

"Syl promotional photo in front of Buckingham fountain in Chicago, IL"

"Syl photoshoot 1970"

"Syl photo material used in tour guide"

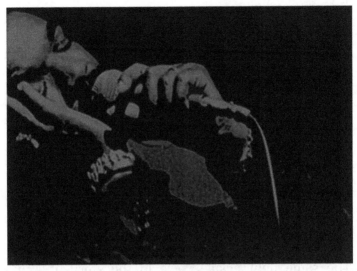

"Syl photo material used on tour"

"Syl's tour lineup released to the public"

Today, artists are keenly aware that they have to check the beats they use in order to assure the beat is truly unique. I don't know if it is laziness or just a lack of care for the original artist that drives them to ignore the beats. Either way, wrongdoing will be called out, especially if its towards me. I feel as strongly about my music being stolen as I do about my family's land. Only acknowledgement and some acres allocated to my family will make it right.

Today, I still battle in court with artists who refuse to accept the facts that they are utilizing a work that was already published. I fight every case like it is my first, because if I don't, no one else will fight for me. The same fight ensues here in the story of Annie Hudson and my family, but the difference is the crooked South has gotten away with taking land from black families for so long and few have fought. There is no attention on the matter, and most people want me and everyone else to walk away and let it go, but how can you let go of your own history? Black people have not escaped slavery if our voices and our rights are not equal. Virginia received everything owed to her by her ancestor, and the black family received nothing. That is blatant racism, which equates to slavism. If I do nothing, then I am not truly free.

Chapter 7

Lost Land

Oxford Bank was caught in a mess. The court had reversed the foreclosure and granted Virginia back her property. The Thompson land was difficult for the bank to offload to any buyer because the chain of title was unclear. All the recorded documents Annie had against the Thompson land were illegal and broke the chain of title. The land was never sold to Annie. Therefore, the Thompsons would still be the proper owners to work with to obtain a transfer of deed. However, none of the brothers were looking to take time out of their day to clear title for a bank that helped to defraud them out of their land! Potential buyers searched for the brothers to clear the deeds, but none of them would accept contact from anyone associated with the property because they were afraid.

The brothers still didn't know they had the right to go after the stolen land. The bank was not forthcoming about the mistakes they made with Annie. They also did not seem to want to correct the errors on their behalf, because that would mean admitting fault. So, Oxford Bank did the only thing they could do. No buyer could get a loan against the property from anywhere but their bank, because they were the only bank that would accept the cloudy title.

Was it because the owners were black?

Marshall County, Mississippi, was known for its outright prejudice towards blacks. Black men who were wealthy were few, and there was no effort to make sure the Thompson family claimed this profitable land. Years later, the land remained a hot potato with the county and the owners. The land had been nicknamed "Cloudy," not just because of the cloudy title associated with it, but also because of the cotton that grew from it. There was no statute for this type of fraud, so the bank and the recorder's office were held to no standard to fix their errors. There was no punishment for stealing land from owners. Similar to the battles with today's squatters, the time and money it takes to prove ownership and rights has put people out of their homes for months and even years.

In 1937, Jay Copper Hurdle, president of First State Bank, went down to Oxford Bank with $2,500 cash and bought the land previously owned by the Thompson brothers. Jay took ownership of the land and began the tedious work of extracting the minerals from the land. Timber deeds and other materials on the land were sold to the highest bidder. Jay stripped the land and left it in limbo until his daughters took it over. The daughters made an effort to get in touch with Joe Thompson in Chicago to get the deeds cleared up. Jay knew the deeds were cloudy and thought that since enough time had passed, his family could work on clearing the title. Although he had this in mind, he himself wanted no part of the decisions on the land. Janice Hurdle took the land and sold it to the Matthews in Memphis, Tennessee. During this time, Owen passed away, and Joe was the only known contact by Jay's family. The deeds on the land remained a mess through all the sales, and no one could seem to get any of the Thompsons to come to the table.

All the land owned by the Thompson brothers sold for $2,500 cash and was stripped of its resources, making Hurdle a little richer than he already was in 1937.

The Bank

Oxford Bank was the only bank at this point capable of lending against the land and transferring to new owners. They were the only ones who had the history of the cloudy title issues. The many loans given to Annie were all drawn on Oxford Bank. The loose lending of the bank and the relationship with Annie came into question with every potential transaction on the property. The bank was known for lending money against properties that the owners couldn't prove was theirs. It was because of banks like Oxford Bank that title insurance grew to be a requirement for closing loans. Chain of title was often broken and hard to trace by banks who continued to lend on titles that were incorrect and owners who were just squatters by definition. In addition, many of the loans prior to title insurance were not being used for land improvements or homes in general. Similar to Annie, the funds were being pulled for personal expenses. Annie, like many others before her, used collateral of land and homes she had no claim to and financed her lifestyle. Annie was somewhat aware of her wrongdoing and that everything would catch up with her, because she relocated to Chicago. She lived a life far from the one she shared with her late husband.

Banks today have an obligation to protect the title of land to insure their own interest in the investment. Although title issues still arise today, title insurance protects the previous and current owners from taking over land that cannot be rightfully transferred. Unfortunately, the Thompson brothers had no such protection during their time. There is a question of how to make the Thompson family whole. Can they be made whole by law?

Chapter 8

Reclamation

Since the time of the Thompson brothers, the land has passed through many hands and many families. It is highly coveted land, large enough to start a separate township and produce income for any owner. Anyone with enough money and ties to the South would want this land, but the avenues of claiming it with clear title are strained. The Thompson brothers were tricked, mistreated, and kicked out of their American dream. They had 642 acres, much more than the forty acres and a mule every slave should have been entitled to after redistribution of land that never happened. So, here is one story of many of those who worked diligently for the land and still ended up with nothing more than a headache.

The Law

Stolen land is not a new topic. Prior to the United States of America becoming what it is today, there were Native Americans living in the lands many of us enjoy. Native American reservations were created to parse out the land. They were forced out of their homes and into designated reservations. Forcing

Native Americans out of their land led to many of them losing their lives. The travel to new areas killed thousands, in addition to the diseases the white settlers exposed the Native Americans to. The lack of vaccination or understanding of the new diseases resulted in many dying. There were also many court cases to pay natives for the land that was claimed for them. One piece of land in particular would give America the Black Hills, located in South Dakota. The Sioux Nation of Native Americans never accepted the money offered for the land, because they had no intent to release their claim on it. Until this day, the money is in the Bureau of Indian Affairs and continues to compound interest, which is now estimated at over one billion dollars.

Slaves were brought to the new world known as America and made slaves in it. Blacks never had a claim to land, other than the promise that the government never came through on after the Civil War. Consequently, land that is bought should be protected at all costs, and the rights of the families must be acknowledged and compensated for if wrongdoing is done. When the rules are followed and the family is black, it seems to be disregarded, which is what this book is bringing to light. It's a sad reminder that land stolen has not been returned to rightful owners. Despite the unforgettable truth of black and brown individuals within America, there is still an obligation to bring light and justice to the losses they have suffered.

Nudd v. Burrows U.S. 426 (1875)

This statute was put in place by a supreme court decision that gives power back to the owners who had property stolen without knowledge. Annie Hudson, being a would-be creditor, broke the law with fraud, forgery, and lies to the government regarding ownership. Ultimately, the Thompson family had no idea land was being foreclosed on for debt that was never owed. Consequently, the 1875 statute should have protected the men and should still do so when challenged today. Presenting the evidence to the courts and determining the right ownership or compensation will set the statute for blacks who step forward to reclaim land of their ancestors. The statue also opens the door to allow questions about the treatment of blacks and whites in the return of land. The reversal from which Virginia Hudson benefited from is the same return that kept the Thompson land away from the families. The legal system is often regarded as unfair, but rarely is there glaring evidence that the court and its officers are committing blatant fraud towards one family over another.

Why You Should Care

Land has been stolen throughout history, and some of it could have been owned by your family. It is no secret that the generational wealth of blacks is limited or nonexistent in many ways. Our communities suffer because we were never given a chance to build. Our equality is still pending delivery to the masses. Yet, we survive through generations, but our survival, which should be now stable and growing, seems to only maintain the status quo. How many more families could have been developed, communities started, businesses owned, billionaires created, or lives saved if we as a people were allowed to flourish in our land with our hard work? The opportunity is available, but it requires some work by the families who have fallen victim to fraud and misconception. This book was created to show the trail of evidence that outlines blatant lies and broken laws that tore a family from their land. We know the truth. Now it is time to march!

Our Next Steps

We are encouraging families to get involved with the Reclamation Foundation! The foundation will lead protests to bring attention to the stolen lands of our ancestors. Money collected by the foundation or land reclaimed will all go back to the families. Where families are not available, it will be given back to the community.

Chapter 9

Evidence

WARRANT DEED (W.D.)

L. B. Hudson

To – Owen Thompson et al

Deed :: For and in consideration of the sum of Twelve Thousand Eight Hundred Dollars ($12,800.00) evidenced by six promissory notes of even date herewith, due and payable respectively one, two, three, four, five and six years after date and for the following amounts:

First - $2261.33, Second - $2398.01, Third - $2541.89, Fourth - $2694.40, Fifth - $2846.06, Sixth - $3016.82, each bearing interest after maturity at the rate of six percent, per annum until paid;

I, L. B. Hudson of Marshall County, Mississippi do hereby convey and warrant unto Owen Thompson, Joe Thompson, Dan Thompson and Will Thompson, the following described real estate, situate, lying and being in Marshall County, Mississippi, to-wit:

All of Section Twenty Four (24) Township Two (2) Range Two (2) West, except two plots of about one acre, each on which is located a burial ground for white people and colored people respectively. Witness my signature this the 8th day of March A.D. 1916.

L. B. Hudson

The State of Mississippi
Marshall County.

Personally appeared before me C. H. Wright Clerk of the Chancery Court in and for said County and State the within named L. B. Hudson who acknowledged that he signed and delivered the foregoing conveyance on the day and year therein mentioned.

Given under my hand and the seal of said Court, this the 8th day of March, 1916.

C. H. Wright-Clerk

Filed for record at 3 P.M. March 8, 1916 and recorded May 29, 1916.

SEAL   Fees .85 Paid   C. H. Wright-Clerk

By J. T. Wade, D.C.

THE STATE OF MISSISSIPPI
MARSHALL COUNTY
I, John W. Taylor, Jr., Clerk of the Chancery Court in and for the State and County aforesaid do hereby certify that the foregoing is a true and correct copy of the original instrument, as fully and completely as the same appears of record in my office. Given under my hand and seal this the _____ day of _____ 19____

JOHN W. TAYLOR, JR. Chancery Clerk

By _____ D.C.

"1916 sale from Hudson to the Thompson brothers."

THE STATE OF MISSISSIPPI, } . Personally appeared before me C.H.Wright Chancery Clerk.
MARSHALL COUNTY.

in and for said County, the within named Owen Thompson-Joe Thompson-Dan Thompson & Will Thompson,
who acknowledged that they signed and delivered the foregoing conveyance on the day and year therein mentioned.
Given under my hand, this 8 day of March 1916

C.H.Wright-Clerk.

THE STATE OF MISSISSIPPI, } Personally appeared before me, the undersigned
COUNTY OF MARSHALL.

in and for said County, the within named

one of the subscribing witnesses to the foregoing instrument, who, being first duly sworn, deposeth and saith that he saw the within named

whose name is subscribed thereto, sign and deliver the same to the said

that he, this deponent, subscribed his name as a witness thereto in the

presence of the said and that he saw the subscribing witness

sign the same in the presence of the said

and that the witnesses signed in the presence of each other on the day and year therein named.

Given under my hand and official seal at office affixed, this day of 191

CLERK'S FEES		THE STATE OF MISSISSIPPI, MARSHALL COUNTY.
Acknowledgment,	$	Filed for record at 3.05 o'clock P M. on the
Filing,	.05	8 day of May 1916
Certificate of Record,	.50	and duly recorded.
Recording......words at 10c per 100		Seal C.H.Wright Clerk.
Total, Paid	$ 2.05	By J.T.Wade D.C.

THE STATE OF MISSISSIPPI Marshall County, Miss.
MARSHALL COUNTY
I, John W. Taylor, Jr., Clerk of the Chancery Court in and for the State and County
aforesaid do hereby certify that the foregoing is a true and correct copy of the original
instrument, as fully and completely as the same appears of record in my office.
Given under my hand and seal this the _____
day of _____ 19__

JOHN W. TAYLOR, JR. Chancery Clerk

By _____ D.C.

"County recorder documents sale to brothers"

DEED OF TRUST ON LAND

FOR AND IN CONSIDERATION of One Dollar to me/us Owen Thompson, Joe Thompson, Dan Thompson & Will Thompson in hand paid by Lester G. Fant, Trustee, and the further consideration hereinafter set out I have bargained, Sold and Conveyed, and these presents do bargain, Sell and Convey to the said Trustee the following property in Marshall County, Mississippi, to wit:
All of Section Twenty Four (24) Township Two (2) Range Two (2) West except two plots of about one acre each, on which is located a burial ground for white people and colored people respectively, according to the plan of said County.

And I warrant the title to said property against the lawful claims of all persons whomsoever; in trust, however, to secure the following indebtedness:
Our joint promissory notes of even date herewith due respectively, one, two, three, four, five and six years after date for the following amounts: first, $2261.33 - second, $2398.01-third, $2541.89 – fourth, $2694.40 – fifth, $2846.06 – sixth, $3016.82, each bearing interest after maturity at the rate of six percent per annum; it being specifically agreed and understood that should default be made in any one of these notes at maturity with all interest then due, that the remaining notes unpaid shall at once become due and payable.

And for any further amounts that may be furnished.
Now, if we shall, on or before the maturity of notes day of next, pay such indebtedness in full, with all interest then due, then this conveyance to be void; but should we fail to pay the same on or before the maturity of notes day of next, or any part thereof, then the said Trustee shall take possession of said property, by himself or agent, and proceed to sell the same, within lawful hours at public sale, to the highest bidder for cash, in front of the south door of the Court House of said County, after having first advertised the time, terms and place of sale as prescribed by Section 2772 of the Mississippi Code of 1906. The proceeds of said sale to be the first applied to the payment of said indebtedness and the making and executing of this trust; the balance, if any, as the law requires.
In case of the death or failure of said Trustee to act, the said L. B. Hudson or any legal holder of said note shall have the power to substitute some other person to execute this trust, by writing under their hand.

WITNESS our hands and seals,   this 8th day of March 1916
                                            His
                              Dan-X-Thompson   Owen Thompson
                                  Mark.   His
                              Will-X-Thompson   Joe-X-Thompson
                                  Mark.   Mark.

"1916 Deed of Trust for sale of land."

Deed of Trust

State of Mississippi}
County of Marshall

Know All Men by These Presents: That, Whereas we, Owen Thompson and wife, Martha Thompson and Joe Thompson and wife Irene Thompson and wife, Hattie Thompson and Will Thompson, widower are indebted to the Federal Land Bank of New Orleans, hereinafter called the Bank, in the sum of Four Thousand and no/100------------Dollars, for money lent by it, which indebtedness and the interest accruing thereon is repayable in Thirty Four (34) fixed annual installments being for Two Hundred Eighty and no/100----------------Dollars, and each subsequent annual installment for the sum of Two Hundred Eighty and no/100----------Dollars, except the last one, which is for One Hundred Thirteen and 60/100-----------Dollars, the first installment being due on the 15th day of October, 1922, and on the same day of each year thereafter until all are paid. Said indebtedness repayable in said fixed annual installments is evidenced by a note of even date herewith for the said principal sum, which, with the interest thereon included, is payable in the amounts and at the times as aforesaid, at the office of the Federal Land Bank of New Orleans, in the City of New Orleans, Louisiana.

AND, WHEREAS, the undersigned desire to secure the payment of said indebtedness as the several installments thereof respectively fall due and the performance of all the obligations, agreements and conditions herein assumed:

NOW, THEREFORE, in consideration of Five Dollars to them paid by Barrett Jones as Trustee, the receipt whereof is hereby acknowledged, the undersigned Owen Thompson and wife Martha Thompson and Joe Thompson and wife Irene Thompson and Dan Thompson and wife Hattie Thompson and Will Thompson, hereinafter called the Grantor, whether one or more, do hereby convey and warrant unto said, Barrett Jones, as Trustee, hereinafter called the Trustee, the following described real estate situated in the County of Marshall, State of Mississippi, to-wit:

All of section Twenty Four (24), Township Two (2), Range Two (2), West, except Two (2) plots of about One (1) acre each on which is located a burial ground for white people and colored people respectively.

"The brothers pay their debt and begin a new loan with the Federal Land Bank of New Orleans"

Will Thompson et al
To – E. M. Smith Trustee
L. A. Rather Exrt of
L. B. Hudson ::

In consideration of One dollar we convey and warrant to E. M. Smith as Trustee the land situated in Marshall County, State of Mississippi, described as All of Section Twenty Four (24) Township Two (2) Range Two (2) West, except two plots of about one acre each on which is located a burial ground for white people and colored people respectively. In trust to secure four (4) notes this day executed by us, each of said notes in the sum of Nineteen Hundred and Forty Seven Dollars and payable to the order of L. A. Rather Sr., as executor of the estate of L. B. Hudson, deceased, or bearer, in one, two, three and four years after date respectively, and each bearing six percent interest from date until paid, it being provided in each of said notes for the payment of all reasonable attorneys fees for collecting it if suit be brought of an attorney be actually employed, the said notes being for balance of purchase money notes for said land executed by us to said L. B. Hudson, now deceased on the 8th day of March, 1916, also to secure all further sums of money which may be advanced or loaned to us or either one of us in the future by the said L. A. Rather Sr., as Executor, of his assignee or assignees of said notes, or any one of them, under the order of the Chancery Court of said County, as may arise from future dealing between the holders or owners of said notes as aforesaid, and ourselves or either one of us, until this instrument is actually marked satisfied upon the margin of its record in the office of the Chancery Clerk of said County.

Now should said notes be paid when due, then this conveyance shall be void, but should the said notes or either or any one of them, not be paid as they respectively fall due, then in any such event all of said notes remaining unpaid at the time shall at once become due and payable whether by their terms they are due of not and the said E. M. Smith, Trustee at the request of the said L. A. Rather Sr., as executor as aforesaid or any legal holder of said notes or any one of them, shall after having first advertises the time, terms and place of sale as prescribed by Section 2772 of the Mississippi Code of 1906 as amended, sell said land within lawful hours, at public outery to the highest bidder for cash in front of the south door of the Court House of said County, shall convey said lands to the purchaser and out of the proceeds of said sale shall pay first the costs of executing this trust, including a reasonable Trustees fee, second the said note or other indebtedness, hereby secured, and the surplus if any as the law directs.

Should the said E. M. Smith Trustee die, decline or become unable from any cause to execute and foreclose this instrument when legally requested then the said L. A. Rather Sr., as Executor aforesaid or any legal holder of said notes or any part of said indebtedness, may in writing duly executed, substituted and appoint some other person as trustee in accordance with Section 2773 or said Code in the place instead of the said E. M. Smith trustee to execute and foreclose this instrument according to the terms and tenor hereof.

Witness our signature this 4th day of October A. D. 1924

Witness J. E. Jones

Will Thompson   X   his mark.
Dan Thompson   X   his mark.
Owen Thompson
Martha Thompson X her mark.
Joe Thompson.
Rena Thompson   X her Mark.

"The new loan is recorded"

The State of Mississippi
County of Marshall

Personally appeared at my office before me, Joseph E. Jones duly qualified and acting Notary Public at the Village of Hudsonville in Supervisors District No. 2 in said County, Owen Thompson and his wife Martha Thompson, Joe Thompson and his wife Rena Thompson, Dan Thompson and Will Thompson, who severally acknowledged that they signed and delivered the forgoing instrument on the day and year therein mentioned.

Given under my hand and official seal affixed, this the 7th day of October, 1924

SEAL   J. E. Jones – Notary Public

Filed for record at 4:45 P.M. October 9, 1924 and duly recorded
SEAL   Fees $1.25   J. T. Wade – Clerk

"Recorder copy of new deed"

Adjustment to Notes

L. B. Hudson,_____)
    Testator (
No. 4787   )
L. A. Rather, Sr. (
    Executor)

Be it remembered that this cause came on this day to be heard before the Chancellor in vacation on the Petition of said executor asking that he be authorized to adjust the three joint notes which cannot be readily collected in full of Owen Thompson, Joe Thompson, Dan Thompson and Will Thompson, each of date March 8th, 1916 and due respectively in four, five and six years from date and each bearing six (6) percent interest from date and the individual note of Will Thompson of date February 17th, 1920 and due December 15th after date and for $1056 and bearing eight (8) percent interest from date and all said notes secured by deed in trust on the land situated in said County of Marshall described as all of Section 24, Township 2, Range 2, West, except two graveyard plots therein described for the burial of white and colored people respectively and said notes aggregating the sum of $7788.00 principal and interest now due, and being for the balance of the purchase money for said land; and it further appearing to the satisfaction of the Chancellor that said land sold now for the liquidation of said notes will not bring by $2000.00 as much as is due thereon and that said debtors are unable to settle said notes, but if indulged all of said notes may be collected; and it further appearing to the satisfaction of the Court that said executor is ready to make his final settlement of said estate and that said notes can be used as distributive shares due said heirs, and that it is to the interest of said heirs and legatees to close up said indebtedness by four equal installments secured by a first lien on said land. It if, therefore ordered, adjudged and decreed by the Chancellor in vacation that said executor be and he is hereby authorized and directed to adjust said notes by taking the four joint notes of said debtors, each said note for the sum of $1947 due respectively in one, two, three and four years from date and bearing six percent interest from date until paid and secured by deed in trust on said land the same to be first lien thereon, said notes to be used as assets in the hands of said executor in making his final settlement herein, said notes to be made payable to said executor or bearer and that said executor make his report of his doings hereunder to the next term of the court, or in his accounting herein.

Ordered, adjudged and decreed this the 3rd day of October, 1924.

_____ _____ ~~Chancellor~~.

~~THE STATE OF MISSISSIPPI~~
~~MARSHALL COUNTY~~
~~I, John W. Taylor, Jr., Clerk of the Chancery Court in and for the State and County aforesaid do hereby certify that the foregoing is a true and correct copy of the original instrument, as fully and completely as the same appears of record in my office. Given under my hand and seal this the ___ day of ___ 19__.~~
~~JOHN W. TAYLOR, JR. Chancery Clerk~~
~~By _____ D.C.~~

"Annie starts making documented claims for the land and money while the Chancellor is on vacation"

Final Decree (Annie Hudson Scheme)

Virginia K. Hudson et al)
No. 5334   Wards (

Mrs. Annie N. Hudson)
        Guardian (

Be it remembered that this cause came on this day to be heard by the Chancellor in vacation on the Petition of the said Mrs. Annie N. Hudson as guardian of and for her said minor children, Annie N. Hudson, Virginia K. Hudson and Dorothy Hudson and the said three minors by their said guardian, and L. A. Rather, Sr., as executor of the estate of L. B. Hudson, deceased, for authority to allow Owen Thompson, Joe Thompson, Dan Thompson and Will Thompson to settle the four notes owed by them to the estate of the said L. B. Hudson, secured by deed in trust on Section 24, Township 2, Range 2, West in Marshall County, Mississippi, by a quit-claim conveyance thereof to the said Mrs. Annie N. Hudson and her said three minor children, and to authorize and direct said guardian to execute an incumbrance or deed in trust upon said land to secure a debt due the said L. A. Rather as set out in said Petition, and the evidence adduced and the Court having heard all of the same, and being now fully advised in the premises, the Chancellor is of the opinion and so finds that the said Petitioners are entitled to the full relief prayed for in their petition as herein granted.

It is therefore ordered, adjudged and decreed that the said Mrs. Annie N. Hudson as guardian of and for her said three minor children Virginia K. Hudson, Annie N. Hudson and Dorothy Hudson and the said L. A. Rather, Sr., as executor of the said L. B. Hudson, deceased, be and they are hereby authorized and empowered and directed to deliver up and return as settled in full to the said Owen Thompson, Joe Thompson, Dan Thompson and Will Thompson, their said four notes each for the sum of $1947.00 and bearing date October 4, 1924 and due respectively in one, two, three, and four years from date, payable to said L. A. Rather as executor and secured by deed in trust upon the said Section of land hereinafter designated, upon the said Owen Thompson, Joe Thompson, Dan Thompson and Will Thompson executing and delivering to the said Mrs. Annie N. Hudson in her own right and to her said minor children, Virginia K. Hudson, Annie N. Hudson and Dorothy Hudson a deed conveying to the jointly share and share alike the said Section Twenty-four (24), Township Two (2), Range Two (2), West, the said deed in trust securing said Thompson Notes to be marked satisfied upon the margin of its record by the said Mrs. Annie N. Hudson as guardian as aforesaid.

It is furthermore ordered, adjudged and decreed that the said Mrs. Annie N. Hudson in her own right and as guardian of the said three minors aforesaid execute and deliver to the said L. A. Rather Sr., a note for the said sum of $2246.33 bearing interest from the 1st day of March, 1925, at the rate of six (6) percent, per annum until paid and due one year after date, which said note shall be secured by deed in trust as an incumbrance on said Section 24, Township 2, Range 2, West, the same being to settle the said amounts paid out by the said L. A. Rather as executor under the order of this Court in said cause No. 4787 and for which said amount said L. A. Rather was holding as security, the said Thompson Notes. The said deed in trust when executed shall be an incumbrance upon said land as provided by Section 2420 of the Code of 1906 as amended in all respects.

Ordered, adjudged and decreed this 18th day of January 1927.

                                    Chancellor.

"No money owed and the Annie scheme begins"

Annie Hudson Scheme (Part II) / In lieu Foreclosure

To the Chancery Court of Marshall County, Mississippi:-

Your Petitioners Annie N. Hudson as guardian of and for her three minor children Virginia K. Hudson, Annie N. Hudson and Dorothy E. Hudson and the said Virginia K. Hudson, Annie N. Hudson and Dorothy Hudson by their said mother the said Annie N. Hudson as their said guardian and L. A. Rather, Sr., as executor of the last will and testament of L. B. Hudson, deceased, all citizens of Marshall County, Mississippi, would respectfully show unto the Court as follows:-

1. That on the 8th day of February, 1922, your said petitioner qualified in this Court as the executor of the last will and testament of L. B. Hudson, who departed this life on the 31st day of January, 1922, having first made and published his last will and testament, which was duly admitted to probate in this Court in Case No. 4787 on the General Docket of said Court, and under the provisions of said will, the said Mrs. Annie N. Hudson, his widow and her three minor children are devised certain portions of said estate. Petitioners will ask to introduce said will as a part of their evidence on the hearing of this said Petition.

2. Petitioners would state that there came into the hands of said L. A. Rather, Sr., as executor of said L. B. Hudson, deceased, certain four joint notes of Owen Thompson, Joe Thompson, Dan Thompson and Will Thompson, each of said notes bearing date October 4th, 1924, and for the sum of $1947.00 and due respectively in one, two, three and four years from date, and secured by first mortgage or deed in trust on Section Twenty-four (24), Township Two (2), Range Two (2), West, being 640 acres more or less and situated in said County of Marshall.

3. That on the 8th day of November, 1924, the said executor filed his Third annual account showing that all probated accounts against said estate had been paid and that he held in his hands certain assets subject to the payments of court costs, attorney's fees and commissions to executor for his trouble and the court on the 13th day of November, 1924 in approving said Third annual account allowed said executor as his commissions to that date the sum of $1000.00 and the attorneys for the estate $800.00 and ordered said executor to dispose of any of said notes at not less that par to raise funds sufficient to pay all said fees, court costs and other expenses of administration. Said executor pledged said Thompson notes for that purpose, but was compelled to take the same up, as said land was not sold and on final settlement which was made and said account approved on the 13th day of November , 1925, the Court ordered him to pay to himself out of said assets as aforesaid, the said Thompson Notes, the said sum of $2246.33, the said executor having theretofore been compelled to take up said borrowed amount and return said Thompson notes to the estate which said amount so paid out by him and due now from said estate amounts to the sum of $2246.33.

4. Petitioners would state that on the 5th day of January, 1927, the said Mrs. Annie N. Hudson qualified in this honorable Court as the guardian of her said three minor children and is now ready to receive from said L. A. Rather, Sr., such parts of the assets as is due said children, but she would state that said assets under the order of the Court stands as pledge for the payment to said Rather the said sum of $2246.33 as aforesaid, so that the same cannot be delivered to her until said amount is paid under the order of the Court, and which is just and should be paid him for the said Court costs and fees paid out by him to relieve the estate of said burden.

5. Petitioners would further show unto the Court that the said Mrs. Annie N. Hudson is interested in said funds or assets to the extent of one fourth interest as one of the legatees of her said deceased husband along with the said three minors in interest, and she is very desirous in so far as she is concerned that the relief herein sought be granted. Petitioners would state and show unto the Court that the said Owen Thompson, Joe Thompson, Dan Thompson and Will Thompson are colored people and live upon said land, that they are poor and never will be able to pay the same out, and one of them has already deserted the premises, that the said debtors are willing to reconvey said land back to the said Mrs. Annie Hudson and her three said minor children upon a surrender to them of the said notes, that said land was sold to the said debtors by the said L. B. Hudson at the time when land values were exceedingly high and cotton was bringing a good price and it was thought they could and would pay for it, but as a matter of fact they cannot do so, thought the said section of land is a fine tract for this section of the Country. The said Mrs. Annie N. Hudson for herself and as guardian of her said three minor children desire that she be authorized to accept a deed from the said Thompson debtors and surrender to them their notes, and that she be authorized to execute a mortgage or incumbrance upon said Section of land for the purpose of raising the amount due the said L. A. Rather as executor,

6. Your said Petitioners aver that the said notes held by the said L. A. Rather, as executor as a part of the assets of said estate are already a lien upon said land in favor of said Rather for the repayment to him of the money advanced to pay said Court costs, in said administration of said L. B. Hudson estate, That a sale of the land now would only be a sacrifice of the same, and a waste of the assets of said estate as land is very low at this time and the price of cotton has rendered it impracticable to attempt a sale of land at public value of the same can be avoided. That the said L. A. Rather, Sr., as executor as aforesaid is perfectly willing to extend the payment of the amount due him for a year or more if the same is secured by a mortgage or incumbrance such as is authorized by law, and they now file this Petition, all parties joining therein and ask that said Mrs. Annie N. Hudson as guardian of the said three minors be authorized to accept the said deed from the said Thompson debtors and that she surrender to them said notes upon the execution of said quit claim deed, and that said guardian of and for her said minor children be authorized and empowered to execute a new incumbrance on said Section 24 to obtain money to pay said L. A. Rather, Sr., or to secure him in the said amount due him as herein set out, the said incumbrance or mortgage to be executed as provided by Chapter 202 of the Laws of 1914 (Hemingway's code Section 1981).

Premises considered the prayer of said Petitioners is that the special relief asked for herein be granted them by the Chancellor in vacation, and as in duty bound your said Petitioners will ever pray, &c.

"Annie moves the property to foreclosure"

In The Chancery Court of Marshall County, Mississippi
In Vacation

BANK OF OXFORD, ET AL - COMPLAINANTS
Vs.   NO. 5697
MRS. ANNE N. HUDSON, ET ALS - DEFENDANTS

Answer of complainants and Cross-Defendants
To Cross-Bill

TO HON. N. R. SLEDGE, CHANCELLOR:-

Come the Bank of Oxford and Phil Stone, Trustee, Complainants in the above styled cause; and file this their answer to the cross-bill filed against them herein, and show unto the Court as follows:-

Cross- Defendants deny that the Defendant Mrs. Anne N. Hudson was not acting for the minor Defendants and Cross-Complainants herein in all of the transactions set out in said answer and Cross-bill but say that in all of said transactions, the said Defendant and cross-Complainant Mrs. Anne N. Hudson was acting not only for herself but for and on behalf of said minor Defendants and Cross-Complainants.

Cross-Defendants further deny that the Defendant Mrs. Anne N. Hudson was deprived of the authority to so act for and on behalf of said minor Defendants by virtue of item third of the Will of L. B. Hudson, deceased, but say that said will of L. B. Hudson, deceased, contains no prohibition or restriction against any of said property being mortgaged.

Complainants and Cross-Defendants further say that the Deed of Trust sought to be foreclosed is not a nullity so far as concerns said minor Defendants and Cross-Complainant but is a good and valid Deed of Trust and a valid lien upon the property of all of the Defendants herein.

Complainants and Cross-Defendants further say that they are entitled to be subrogated to the lien held by L. A. Rather Sr., which was paid off by Complainant and Cross-Defendant Bank of Oxford on March 1, 1925, in the amount of $_____, plus $_____interest, a total of principal and interest in the amount of $_____, since said lien of said L. A. Rather Sr. was a valid lien duly fixed on Section 24, Township 2, Range 2, West, Marshall County, Mississippi. Complainants and Cross-Defendants further say that it has been necessary to place the notes secured by the Deed of Trust in the hands of attorneys for collection and that Complainants and Cross-Defendants are entitled to an attorney's Fee in the amount of $_____.

Complainants and Cross-Defendants say that in all events, they are certainly entitled to a lien on the interest of all of the Defendants in said Section 24, Township 2, Range 2, West, Marshall County, Mississippi, as above set out and that they are certainly entitled to a lien upon all of the individual interest of Defendant Mrs. Anne N. Hudson in all of said property conveyed in said Deed of Trust which is hereby sought to be foreclosed.

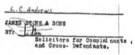

L. C. Andrews

JAMES STONE & SONS
BY:
Solicitors for Complainants
and Cross- Defendants.

"Annie goes head to head with the bank claiming rights to property"

To —wit:

All the interest of Mrs. Anne N. Hudson, Virginia K. Hudson, Anne Hudson and Dorothy Hudson in and to Section 24, Township 2, Range 2, West, same being all of said section 24, Township 2, Range 2, West, except two acres heretofore conveyed for church property; also the interest of Mrs. Anne N. Hudson in and to the North half of Section 34, the west one half of the South East Quarter of Section 35, the East end or side of the South West Quarter of Section 26, being 120 acres, and the North West fraction of the North East Quarter of Section 35, being 85 acres, more or less, all of said lands being in Township 2, Range 2, West.

The consideration for all the interest of Mrs. Anne N. Hudson, Virginia K. Hudson, Anne Hudson and Dorothy Hudson in and to said section 24, Township 2, Range 2, West, except two acres heretofore sold for church property, was $3,050.00, and the consideration for the interest of Mrs. Anne H. Hudson in and to the other described land was $3,400.00 making a total consideration o $6,550.00 for all of the above described lands.

Witness my signature, this the 19th day of July, A.D. 1932

L. C. Andrews, Commissioner

STATE of MISSISSIPPI
COUNTY of MARSHALL

Before me the undersigned authority this day personally appeared L. C. Andrews, Commissioner, who acknowledged that he signed and delivered the above and foregoing instrument on the day and year therein mentioned, and for the purposes therein stated.

Given under my hand and official seal of office, this the 19th day of July, A.D. 1932

S. V. Cochran, Chancery Clerk

By: H. K. Mahon, D.C.

SEAL

Filed for record at 8 A.M. on the 2nd day of August, 1932 and duly recorded.

S. V. Cochran, Chancery Clerk

"Annie claims money is owned to her"

LAND DEED RECORD No. 79, MARSHALL COUNTY, MISSISSIPPI

Bank of Oxford
TO: The Republic Creosoting Co. Inc.:
TIMBER DEED

Know All Men By These Presents, That Bank of Oxford, a corporation organization and created under and by virtue of the laws of Mississippi, domiciled in Oxford, Lafayette County, said State, for and in consideration of the sum of Eight Hundred Dollars ($800.00) cash in hand paid, the receipt of which is hereby acknowledged, does by these presents, sell, convey and warrant to Republic Creosoting Company, Inc., all merchantable timber and merchantable timber like trees, except the chestnut timber, standing lying and being in and upon the land described as follows, to wit:

Section 24, Township 2, Range 2, containing 638 acres, more or less, situated, lying and being in Marshall County, State of Mississippi. Together with full right, at any time hereafter, to enter, cut, remove and otherwise, at pleasure utilize same and also right of way there over to locate, construct, maintain, use and remove roads and bridges and all other instrumentalities and appliances, at pleasure, on over, through and across same for all aforesaid purposes and any other by grantee deemed proper, and the erect, maintain thereon and remove there from all such structures as may be requisite in such operation.

Grantee in enjoying the rights hereunder shall not injure or damage the crops, stock and fences thereon or other property of the grantor.

It is expressly agreed that the grantee will remove said merchantable timber and merchantable timber like trees within two years from this date.

In witness whereof said Bank of Oxford has caused these presents to be signed by G. F. Heard, President and J. T. Davis, Cashier this the 24th day of March, 1937.
Bank of Oxford
By: G. F. Heard, President
J. F. Davis, Cashier
SEAL

STATE OF MISSISSIPPI
LAFAYETTE COUNTY
Personally appeared before me, Ruby McCoy a Notary Public in and for the county and state aforesaid, G. F. Heard and J. T. Davis who are personally known to me, and who acknowledged that they, as President and Cashier respectively, of and for and behalf, and by authority of Bank of Oxford, a corporation organized under the laws of Mississippi, domiciled in Oxford, Lafayette County, Mississippi, signed and the above and foregoing instrument and affixed the corporate seal of said Bank of Oxford thereto and delivered said instrument on the day and year therein mentioned

Given under my hand and official seal of office, this the 24th day of March, A.D., 1937
SEAL   Ruby McCoy, Notary Public
My Commission expires Sept. 24, 1940

Filed for record at 10 A.M. on the 3rd day of April, 1937 and duly recorded
S. V. Cochran, Chancery Clerk

"Land is stripped of Timber by new owners"

Bank of Oxford :: (Outrageous Sale) To J. Cooper Hurdle

Bank of Oxford:
To:
J. Cooper Hurdle:

Know All Men By These Presents, that Bank of Oxford, Oxford, Mississippi, a banking corporation organized and existing under the laws of the state of Mississippi does by these presents, for and in consideration of Twenty Five Hundred Dollars ($2500.00) cash in hand paid, the receipt of which is hereby acknowledged, sell, convey and warrant to J. Cooper Hurdle the following described tract, lot or parcel of land situated, lying and being in Marshall County, Mississippi, to wit: -

Section 24, Township 2, Range 2, West, except two acres heretofore sold for Church property.

It is understood and agreed that said land is rented for the year 1937, and that the rent for the place for said year of 1937 do not pass by this instrument to the grantee herein, but are expressly reserved unto the grantor herein.

In Witness whereof said Bank of Oxford, has caused these presents to be signed by its president and cashier thereunto duly authorized and its corporate seal be hereunto affixed, this the 28th day of July, A.S. 1937.

SEAL

STATE OF MISSISSIPPI
LAFAYETTE COUNTY.

Bank of Oxford

By G. F. Heard, President

By J. T. Davis, Cashier

Before me the undersigned authority this day personally appeared G. F. Heard and J. T. Davis, who are personally known to me, and who acknowledged that they, the said G. F. Heard as President and J. T. Davis as Cashier of and for and on behalf of Bank of Oxford, a banking corporation organized and existing under the laws of the state of Mississippi, signed the above and foregoing instrument and affixed the corporate seal of said Bank of Oxford thereto and delivered said instrument on this day and year therein mentioned.

Given under my hand and official seal of office, this the 28th day of July, A.D. 1937,

{SEAL}

Ruby McCoy, Notary Public

Filed for record at 4p.m. on the 10th day of August, 1938 and duly recorded.

S. V. Cochran

"Land sold to J Hurdle Cooper for only $2500"

THOMPSON's Land Reclamation Foundation
Tracking Sheet/Title Search

MARSHALL COUNTY, MISSISSIPPI

SECTION 24 TOWNSHIP 2 RANGE 2 W

GRANTOR	GRANTEE	DATE	Book	Page	KIND	N.E. ¼	N.W. ¼	S.W. ¼	S.E. ¼	ACR.
U.S.A.	A. Chuck A Tubby	01-25-1836	Index		O.E.	All	All	All	All	
A. Chuck A. Tubby	H. Anderson & E. Orne		A	207	W.D.	All	All	All	All	
Edward Orne	H. Anderson	01-10-1839	F	182	P.A.	All	All	All	All	
Henry Anderson	A. M. Clayton	11-25-1842	K	342	W.D.	All	All	All	All	
J. C. Alderson Commr.	H. Anderson	12-26-1842	L	463	Commr.	All	All	All	All	
A. M. Clayton etux	C. T. Hudson	07-04-1845	N	51	W.D.	All	All	All	All	
Mary S. Hudson	John L. Hudson	12-01-1852	S	141	W.D.	Int. in All	Int.	Int.	Int.	
John L. Hudson etux	Houston & Reeves	09-20-1867	27	103	W.D.	All	All	All	All	
Jas. S. Stephens	John C. Atkison Tr.	01-14-1871	31	255	D.T.				60A.	
T. W. Reeves etal	J. L. Hudson	01-20-1880	46	633	W.D.	All	All	All	All	
John L. Hudson	Edwin Gholson Tr.	03-26-1883	48	137	D.T.	All	All	All	All	
John L. Hudson	Hammond & Hall Tr.	05-23-1892	57	228	D.T.	All	All	All	All	
John L. Hudson Sr.	L. B. Hudson	11/30/1910	72	194	W.D.	All	All	All	All	
Owen Thompson etal	L. G. Fant Tr.	3/8/1916	7	260	D.T.	All	All	All	All	
L. B. Hudson	Owen Thompson etal	3/8/1916	73	570	W.D.	All less 2A.	All	All	All	
Will Thompson	B. R. Cheairs Tr.	3/30/1918	7	570	D.T.	Und. Int.	Und. Int.	Und. Int.	Und. Int.	
Owen Thompson etal	Marshall County	9/2/1919	74	487	W.D.				R/W	
DO	Barrett Jones Tr.	10/15/1921	9	41	D.T.	All	All	All	All	
Owen Thompson etal	E. M. Smith Tr.	3/29/1924	11	252	D.T.	All less 2A.	All	All	All	
Will Thompson etal	DO	10/4/1924	10	325	D.T.	DO	DO	DO	DO	
Owen Thompson etal	Mrs. Annie N. Hudson	1/3/1927	76	496	W.D.	All less 2A.	All	All	All	
Annie N. Hudson etal	H. H. Rather Tr.	1/28/1927	13	98	D.T.	All less 2A.	All	All	All	
Lynn B. Hudson	S. A. Winborn Tr.	5/14/1928	13	299	D.T.	All Int. in	All Int. in	All Int. in	All Int. in	640
Ann N. Hudson etal	Phil Stone Tr.	5/21/1929	13	471	D.T.	All	All	All	All	
L. C. Anderson Commr.	Bank of Oxford	7/19/1932	77	531	Comr. Deed	All	All	All	All	
R. C. Houston et al	Anna Houston, Armour	3/3/1934	78	145	Q.C.D.				Error	
Bank of Oxford	Republic Creosoting Co.	3/24/1937	79	532	Timber Deed	All	All	All	All	
Bank of Oxford	J. Cooper Hurdle	7/28/1937	80	372	W.D.	All	All	All	All less 2 A Church lot.	
J. Cooper Hurdle	State Hwy. Comm/Miss.	2/22/1940	81	374	W.D.				R of W.	
J. Cooper Hurdle	John R. McKinnie	5/22/1945	4	43	O & G Lease	All	All	All	All less 9 A.	
J. C. Hurdle	H.M. & D.A. Wilson	6/17/1949	4	107	O & G Lease	All	All	All	All less 9 A.	
Mrs. J. C. Hurdle	Luther F. Matthews	1/19/1967	111	445	W.D.	All	All	All	All less R of W.	
Luther F. Matthews	Sidney L. Hurdle Tr.	1/19/1967	53	81	D.T.	All	All	All	All less R of W Hwy 7.	
Janie J. Hurdle	Luther F. Matthews	2/11/1969	59	352	Release					
Hackamore Ranch	Oxford Prod. Credit Assoc	8/19/1974	87	55	L.D.T.	All Land Lying in Sect. 22, 23, 24.				
L.F. Matthews Hackamore F	Oxford Prod. Credit Assoc	8/19/1974	87	96	D.T.	All Land Lying in Sect. 22, 23, 24.				
Hackamore Ranch Ex & Tr.	Oxford Prod. Credit	2/18/1977	96	585	D.T.	All Land				
The est/Luther Matthew	Oxford Prod Credit Assoc.	2/18/1977	98	2	D.T.					642
Hackamore Ranch, Matt.est	Oxford Prod. Credit	9/22/1978	104	20	D.T.	All of Land Lying in this Section.				
	VOID	VOID	VOID	VOID	VOID	VOID				

SECTION 24 TOWNSHIP 2 RANGE 2 ACREAGE 641.54

Page 2

THOMPSON's Land Reclamation Foundation
Tracking Sheet/Title Search

MARSHALL COUNTY, MISSISSIPPI

Section 24 Township 2 Range 2 W

GRANTOR	GRANTEE	DATE	Book	Page	KIND	DESCRIPTION
Hackamore Ranch	Oxford Prod. Credit	10/25/1979	108	656	D.T.	All See Book and page
Hackamore Ranch	Oxford Prod. Credit	10/25/1979	110	154	D.T.	
Hackamore Ranch	Oxford Prod. Credit Asso.	10/29/1980	112	386	D.T.	All 640 A. less 7 A.
Harold Matthew et al	Gustin Raikos & Matthew	10/4/1982	189	157	Sp. W.D.	All Less Pt.

"a depiction of our land changes hands after
100 years of fraud"

Annie Hudson
by Syl Johnson

Annie Hudson,

Beautiful woman

But you had ways like your no-good ass man

Annie Hudson, Annie Hudson

Beautiful woman

But you had ways like your no-good man

She took my grandfather and his three brothers'
homes and she ran

Annie Hudson

Beautiful woman

Had ways like her no-good ass man

Annie Hudson

Beautiful woman

But she had ways like her no-good ass man

She made a funky move down in Mississippi

Took my grandfather and brothers' whole section
of land

Section 24 Township 2 range to Marshall County,
Mississippi

Don't need a description

Don't need a description of my grandfathers and his three brothers' land

She made a funky move in Mississippi She had a massive plan?

Annie Hudson

Beautiful

Annie Hudson

Said she went both ways

Annie Hudson

They said she went both ways

Yes, she did

When she came out the closet

She came out the closet to stay

Annie Hudson

Man wanna hit it

Had enough money

He always could

Annie Hudson

Man wanna hit it

Had enough money

He always could

When she came out the closet

When she came out the closet, ya know

She came out the closet for good

Annie Hudson

Annie Hudson

Annie Hudson

Annie Hudson Would you Mississippi?

Bishop Mississippi?

Reclaim Foundation

The Reclaim Foundation was put in place to assist families who have been torn from their land to help fight to get it back. Founded by Syl Johnson in 2019, the foundation intends to reunite families with their history and where possible with the land that belongs to them. If you have a story to tell, contact the foundation.

Our Purpose:

Capture an understanding of land owned by slaves

List of stolen land

Reclamation efforts

Resources and partners

Legal volunteers Contact us by Mail:

RECLAIM!

3473 S. Martin Luther King Dr.

Suite 506

Chicago, IL 60616

About the Author

"Syl Live in Russia"

Syl Johnson is a Grammy-nominated blues singer/songwriter and producer that has captured audiences across the globe for decades with his soulful and unique voice. His career spans more than sixty years. Born in Holly Springs, Mississippi, in 1936, Syl came from a family of musicians and singers. This legacy extended to his five children, nine grandchildren, and ten great-grandchildren with their own gifts and talents, succeeding both in their careers and at school. Syl makes it known that he wants to leave behind generations of wealth, longevity, and prosperity for his family years after he has gone.

Syleena Johnson, his youngest daughter, is a Grammy-nominated R&B singer-songwriter also known for being one of the hosts of the TV One daytime talk show *Sister Circle* since late 2017. She has also made appearances on other shows such as Iyanla's *Fix My Life* and starred in TV One's reality series *R&B Divas: Atlanta*. Syleena quickly made a name for herself outside of her father's name by working with popular acts like Busta Rhymes, Common, Kanye West, and a reggae collaboration album with Musiq Soulchild called *9ine*. She often sites her father being an inspiration for much of her music, having helped jumpstart her career, and she has worked with him on several projects. They have a joint album called *This Time Together* by Father Daughter that was released in 1995. Syleena's 2017 studio album, *Rebirth of Soul*, was produced by Syl.

Syl quickly found his passion for music, with his two brothers, Jimmy Johnson and Mack Thompson, who had their hands in music as well. With roots in Chicago from the 1950s, Syl used his talents to play alongside the likes of notable blues artists such as Junior Wells and Howlin' Wolf. Quickly making a name for himself in the Chicago blues scene, Johnson became the breakout star of the label Twinight Records, formerly known as Twilight Records, in the mid1960s, eventually going on to produce many of the label's songs. With hits like "Different Strokes," "Take Me to the River," "Is It Because I'm Black," and "Come on, Sock It to Me," Syl's influence is still felt today in music.

Syl's talents have led him to perform all around the world in countries like Australia, Turkey, and Greece. Johnson is one of the most sampled artists in history, with samples that span across several genres and years. In the late eighties, there was a rise in the sampling of Syl's music. During this time, Johnson became regarded as the first black chain restaurant owner in downtown Chicago. The restaurant, Solomon's Fishery, became well known in the community for its healthier options and approach to soul food. Syl sought to benefit and uplift urban communities with the organic recipes used throughout his restaurants. With the success of Solomon's Fishery rising, Syl expanded to other parts of the country with his restaurant. With locations in Indiana and Georgia, he began to find success in retirement with his chain of restaurants across the US.

Discovering that people were recognizing and sampling his music, Johnson began seeking out the songs and artists using his music. His journey of receiving the respect and credit he was due in the music industry, brought Syl briefly out of retirement to release a new album in the early nineties called *Back in the Game*, even collaborating with his daughter Syleena on this album. A man passionate about his legacy, artistry, and music, he took it in his own hands to sue notable artists such as Kanye West, The Go! Team, Public Enemy, and Jay Z, who had used his songs without proper credit or permission. With the success of many hit songs sampling Syl's music, even a Grammy nomination for the *Watch the Throne* joint album by Kanye West and Jay Z, the fight in Syl for his legacy and respect was sparked.

Many of these stories are told in the 2015 documentary *Any Way the Wind Blows*. Premiering at the Chicago Film Festival, the documentary was well received by critics, as well as new and longtime fans of Syl. Throughout 2015–16, it won various awards, including Best Documentary Feature Audience Award at Indie Memphis and SF IndieFest, Gibson Music Films/Music City Grand Jury Prize at the Nashville Film Festival, Saatchi & Saatchi Nothing is Impossible Achievement Award at the Martha's Vineyard African American Film Festival, and Documentary Jury Prize at the Sidewalk Film Festival.

His personal story of triumph in the music industry and the fight for getting the respect and credit he worked for continues to inspire many. That same fight is seen in Syl's creation of a reclamation of stolen land foundation.

Learn more about Syl's foundation by writing:

RECLAIM!

3473 S Martin Luther King Dr.

Suite 506

Chicago, IL 60616